Depression Investor

VINCE CARRAWAY

authorHOUSE®

AuthorHouse™
1663 Liberty Drive
Bloomington, IN 47403
www.authorhouse.com
Phone: 1-800-839-8640

First published by AuthorHouse 1/8/2010

ISBN: 978-1-4490-6527-0 (e)
ISBN: 978-1-4490-6526-3 (sc)

Library of Congress Control Number: 2009913960

Printed in the United States of America
Bloomington, Indiana

This book is printed on acid-free paper.

THIS BOOK IS DEDICATED TO

"HUCKLEBERRY" & "BUTTERFLY"

MY TWO GRANDCHILDREN

Contents

Introduction

Anxiety, accompanied by deprivation, leads to hoarding. You can take that to the bank. When I was a youngster, I would always listen to my parent's generation talk about the "Great Depression." This was a stark contrast to the era of the 50's when I was growing up. The 1930's Depression era piqued my interest in economics that has lasted a lifetime and I want to share my learning experience with my grandchildren. I never felt poor or in any way deprived during my early years, but found the depression of the 30's fascinating. There were several theories that came to light, but I could never really fully understand it.

Recently, in 2008, we had reached a point in time where we were on the verge of a financial collapse of our monetary system that we haven't seen in 70 years. This writing highlights the people and situations of the mortgage and investment banking system that played havoc with our entire monetary base. There are many more hard working, honest people in the financial world that played no part in the 2008 financial collapse but still lost their jobs. Some people worked in areas of business that were not even remotely connected to the mortgage industry and were innocently damaged by its downdraft. There were also some people whose fraud was exposed as Ponzi schemes when the real estate bubble burst, as all bubbles finally do.

Home ownership is the Rock of Gibraltar of our culture. It is what every family aspires to. Home ownership was regulated and controlled by two federal organizations called Fannie Mae and Freddie Mac. When you wanted to take out a mortgage you went to your local bank and applied for a loan or mortgage. There were strict rules as what percentage you had to put up for a down payment and how to prove your ability to pay additional housing expenses on a monthly basis. Simple enough, the mortgages were then bought usually by Freddie and/or Fannie with a positive result for all parties. Homeowners paid their mortgages, the banks did well and Freddie Mac and Fannie Mae did their job.

The problem came after Freddie and Fannie started to fall into administrative disarray. The politicians in Washington were pushing for more home ownership and advocated new ways or instruments for this to be achieved. This book deals with only the narrow band of people in the business community that rocked the very fiber of our culture.

There was a trillion dollar mortgage industry that was totally unregulated and involved millions of American homeowners. So you now had mortgage originators (i.e., people writing mortgages) that joined forces with an unregulated Wall Street. Wall Street brokerage houses had become investment banks with access to the savings accounts of millions of Americans. What became an explosion in the center of the housing bubble was when an unregulated Wall Street met unregulated mortgage originators.

Collateralized Debt Obligations are many mortgages that are wrapped together to form a package. In these packages are mortgages of various credit worthiness. Some were sub prime mortgages with questionable ability to pay. These packages were randomly grouped together and sold, with 50% sold abroad by Wall Street. When too much bad debt or sub prime mortgages are laced with the good payer mortgages the package starts to fragment because of default on payments. When you have many packages starting to fail you have a disaster waiting to happen and it did.

Credit default swaps are bets issued by financial institutions that people will default on mortgage payments and the value of these mortgage packages will go down.

What I want to convey is a deductive reasoning experience that will be a guidepost to investing for young adults and novice investors.

I hope that you may learn from my mistakes, successes and observations.

Chapter 1

"Free market capitalism is the best pathway to prosperity"------ Larry Kudlow (1)

1957 - Increased unemployment and loss of jobs for my friend's parents

Oct. 1957 Sputnik launched

The race is on . U.S. vs. Russia

Big push for science and math

New York State teachers colleges offered NO tuition for full time students registered in a teaching program. - any teaching program.

The best and brightest and hardest working entered programs like medicine, chemistry, pharmacy, engineering, aerospace, physics and mathematics. Those that couldn't do these programs went on to become business majors. Competition was stiff among these science and math students. One of my firm beliefs is that real college is science and math and it's not where you go to school, but what you take.

My roommate and I were both chemistry majors for the first semester of our freshman year. By the second semester, I switched to bio major with a science minor (chemistry and physics). I was finally on track for my way to graduate school goals. My roommate went on probation.

He was a smart person, but not focused. By the end of the second semester he was told that he must switch out of science to a much easier program such as business. He did switch his major to business and became an A student without much effort. Now these were the days prior to most MBA degrees. We roomed together for several more undergraduate years. It all went pretty much the same - me taking classes in the morning and taking long labs in the afternoon until 4-6p.m. He would take three hours of classes per day at the maximum, go home right after lunch, take a nap, maybe look over some reading in his business program for ½ hour, leave for an early dinner and go out for the evening, sometimes crossing paths as he was going out and I was arriving home just to begin a long night of study after a quick dinner. I remember one night we crossed paths on the front porch of the rooming house where we lived. I was taking comparative anatomy and dissecting the shark. I had my shark specimen and had it thoroughly wrapped and was carrying it under my arm when we crossed paths. I always stored my shark in the basement of our rooming house in a sealed container. When we crossed paths on the front porch of our residence, my roommate pointed to the entourage following me. Apparently I did not seal my shark specimen well enough and there was a group of cats following me. We had a great laugh over that. At that point my roommate told me since it was Thursday night he was going to be studying about two hours for his Friday business quizzes. This became somewhat of a ritual for my roommate - two hours of study on Thursday night for Friday quizzes and that was pretty much the extent of it. This amount of effort yielded pretty much A grades for the remaining three years. He came back for graduate school in business (education) and again followed the same game plan with great success. I had gone on to graduate school in science. He taught business in high school until he was draft deferred at age 26 (remember this was during the Vietnam War), then worked on Wall Street for several years. The last I heard from him was that he left New York and moved to Chicago to work at the Commodities Exchange. That was pretty much the pattern of the times. Those that could went on to some form of math and science, those that couldn't went on to business. This chronological group was from prior to WWII, during WWII, and the very beginning of the Baby Boomer generation.

When investing money, one has to know that Bernie Madoff was of that age group and many "ain't that smart". Oh sure, Warren Buffett is very smart and I even invest with him (B shares of course). There are always exceptions to the rule and many of them, but the general trend is what I have just mentioned. I have a dear friend (M.D.) who went to a class reunion at a prestigious university. He returned to tell me that he couldn't believe how much money some of his classmates donated to his under graduate alma mater. I told him I knew a lot about his classmates. He laughed and blew me off. I told him that probably all were business majors. He pondered and, in amazement, told me I was absolutely right. I then really dumbfounded him by telling him that some of those classmates had started in math and science and changed to a business major because it was much less rigorous. He pondered and again, with reluctance, admitted I was correct. At that point I didn't want to endanger our friendship so I said goodbye and left.

Be careful who you give your money to. They may not be as smart as you think. In the financial world, with a little bit of luck, you can be rather mediocre and become very wealthy. The intellectual competition was not all that great. I think that if you watched the market meltdown in 2008 and early 2009, especially on television, you will note that this really speaks to the point I am trying to make. Most of the pundits were in a state of total confusion and were so far removed from Main Street that they became hogtied and missed the boat when the tsunami came. No one listened to Prof. Nouriel Roubini, Peter Schiff, John Tice, Prof. Ravi Batra and most of all Robert Shiller ("Irrational Exuberance"). Sometimes they are too pessimistic but they provide a modicum of reality. The housing market is a prime example of the know-nothing, stupid belief that the value and cost of housing was going to continually rise forever. Cannot one see that the job market is shrinking and that the salaries do not match up with rising cost of homes? We lived in a very modest house in what used to be "out in the country." With suburban sprawl, we were no longer as private. I did, however, notice that homes that were being built were of the "Mc Mansion" variety and I always said that the job market where we lived did not support this kind of lifestyle for the huge number of people that were building them. This was just plain old common sense 4-5 years prior to the meltdown.

Politicians and financial geniuses tend to live in such Mc Mansions and they surround themselves with people just like themselves, then they all converse about how smart each other is. They are not in touch with Main Street.

I always think of the movie "Bronx Tale" where the Don, played by Chaz Palminteri, says to the youngster he has taken under his wing, "I could afford to live anywhere, but I stay in the old neighborhood so I can always know what is really going on." (availability). Chaz says this, or something similar to this, as he drives his Cadillac backwards on a one way street from his home to his place of business.

Now Chaz's character doesn't have an MBA but great common sense. One cannot drift far from regular people to see the economic landscape. The middle class, as our parents knew it, is disappearing fast. Trickle-down economics does not work when you lose the next level down -- the middle class -- which directly or indirectly has its roots in manufacturing. In manufacturing there are various levels of skills with various grades of salaries commensurate with the gradation of skills. Trickle-down economics will work here just as it did during Reagan's administration. The proponents of this fail to acknowledge that this will not work in a two class service industry. In our present small business economy there are one, two, or at most, several skilled people or bosses at the top. The next level is minimum wage or slightly above minimum wage workers. It basically is a two level work force without a lot of money changing hands between the two levels. Here is where trickle down economics does not work. The only things that trickle are the crumbs. The gradation of highly skilled, to skilled, to semi-skilled, to labor only, are all lost and so are the commensurate salaries.

I can remember as a kid I always liked to pass by manufacturing plants and view the many different autos in the lots. I always thought that the better the job you had was measured by the car you drove. In other words, there were some expensive cars for the bosses, next some more moderate costing cars and so on down the line. What I can distinctly remember was that there was a vast gradation in the prices of the cars in the lot. Now, in retrospect, I realize that these cars represented the wide array of skill levels in manufacturing and thus the various pay levels.

With the advent of both legal and illegal immigration, especially from Mexico, many of the hourly workers already here have suffered greatly in economic advancement. What I really cannot understand is how the politicians and corporate executives sold the entire Hispanic community on the idea that uncontrolled immigration is good. We have been taking advantage of these hardworking people and place them in a situation where it is going to take them twice as long to assimilate. Why not control immigration and give them a chance to work at a better wage, not having to look over their shoulder at every turn. This was one of the greatest faux pas ever. Cut manufacturing in America -- use this to keep wages lower. Then you allow in a multitude of even cheaper labor to work at unlivable wages -- indentured servants if you will. Then you sell to the Hispanic community the idea of open borders and free trade (of course at poverty wages) and obtain all of their support and votes. The politicians get re-elected, the corporate executives get fat, the American workers in the defunct middle class get poorer, the illegals are forced into a situation of economic servitude, the corporate executives leverage their companies to the hilt to show a false rise in value of their stock. The executives sell their options, take their golden parachutes and move their money out of the country to the Cayman Islands. What a snow job. Of course, we have failed to mention the lobbyists and their piece of the action. The shareholders, in the past, used to gain something from this, but that isn't even true anymore. With this as a format we will never be able to solve the immigration problem and give these poor people an opportunity to earn a good living. Who said business majors ain't smart. There will be more about indentured servants from the educational industrial military complex later on.

(1) Daily on CNBC television show "Kudlow & Company"

Chapter 2

Onward now to grad school in the mid 60's. Ah yes, I lived in graduate housing - one of 20,000 plus grad students. Low and behold, two of my neighbors and good friends-to-be were in M.B.A. programs. Now, this was an evolution of my poor attitude toward business majors. These were Masters in Business Administration, but there was a cute twist on this program which was supposed to be rated as one of the top 10 or 12 at that time. The twist was that these people all had undergraduate degrees in math or science. All of the people already had science, math or engineering degrees. They took this program as an adjunct to their existing degrees. Since the undergrad school did not have a business program, all emphasis in business was at the MBA level. This was when people took jobs and stayed a rather long time in the same field.

So as you probably figured out by now, the MBA was mostly designed to be a stepping stone for technical people (those of math and science) to become better managers as they climbed the corporate ladder. Since many of these people stayed in the same field or with the same company for a long time, it behooved corporations to finance these MBA programs. Well, you know the American way - if a little bit is good, a deluge is much better. So now we have MBA programs starting to spring up all over the place. Now you recall the quote "it's not where you go to college, but what courses you take" - well, that was for math and science programs. For MBA programs it was where you went to business school. School prestige was everything. At first, the top schools entered the competition. Now they have to fill their coffers with this corporate tuition money. But what is the educational military industrial complex to do? We don't have enough mathematicians and scientists to fill all of these programs. They are going to lose this big tuition money - both corporate and student loan money. These MBA programs should certainly charge more tuition than mere undergrad programs. Lo and behold we will bypass the technical, math and science people and start accepting people with undergraduate degrees in business. We will bypass the technical people and sell the idea that anyone could be a boss by taking their particular MBA program. In other words we will teach students to manage people, not a product. We will create high powered business chieftains that can go from company to company just by managing people and bottom line not really understanding the underlying business.

So you have people running auto tire companies and then running an electronics company. Ken Langone paid a lot of money to Robert Nardelli to run Home Depot. He then paid a lot of money to buy out the rest of Nardelli's contract and now Robert Nardelli is CEO of Chrysler. Where is Chrysler going to end up? No one knows. Observing Robert Nardellis' segue from Home Depot to Chrysler, I merely use this as an example to illustrate that home renovations and construction is a far cry from the manufacturing of automobiles.

Now to continue with managing of people - IBM was known never to lay off a worker until 1993. IBM was also known to promote from within the company. Many of their managers did not have college degrees, they were high school grads that grew into management positions by understanding the culture of the company. This served IBM well and lasted many years until just recently. Now this evolution of the MBA's from undergrad technical to undergrad business majors took a long time. Remember the Dow Jones Industrial Average languished from 1966 to 1982. There was a slower rate of conversion than after 1982. There were not the propellants that occurred after 1982 to increase the demand of the MBA degree.

During July of 1969, we landed a man on the moon. At that point the scientific race seemed to be over. It was like, we won and math and science did not seem to be as important as it once was. We avenged Sputnik.

I know of one broker who lied about having a college degree to qualify for the first brokerage job and wound up ultimately founding their own brokerage firm.

I know of one mutual fund manager who had dropped out of premed because it was too rigorous, went to business school, and ran a successful mutual fund for awhile. He then started his own firm which he ultimately sold for several hundred million dollars.

I think you get the picture. You really have to be careful who you give your money to. Many are not that smart.

Hedge funds do not have as much regulation as mutual funds. According to "Dateline" on CBS television, hedge fund manager Sam Israel never graduated from Tulane University as he would have liked to have his clients believe. He squandered millions of his clients money and ultimately landed in jail. There is a lot of money to be made in hedge funds, but the risk is very great. These are not for most investors. Remember, you and I are depression investors. We have to be careful who we invest our money with. Presently we have ETF's, exchange traded funds. These are baskets of funds that represent various sectors of the stock market. XLE, for example, represents various stocks in the oil industry. This gives you a smattering of the oil industry, are low cost, and can be traded like a stock. ETF's are a low cost way to get representation in various sectors of the stock market.

Chapter 3

During 1982 and the early Reagan administration, the stock market started its upward trend. The environment for business growth and stocks was favorable, trickle down economics was working because we had a solid middle class. There was also an interest in saving for retirement. In the late 1960's, I believe 1967, the Keough Plan was introduced for self-employed people. This allowed someone that worked for themselves to place money in a tax deferred account. There were rules regarding maximum contributions but, hey, it was a great idea and a great start. Now many that started with this, and if they were in stocks, got hurt in 1974 after the S&P index dropped 30%. But with a portfolio with stocks and a good percentage of bonds, most survived if they stayed with their holdings. The key to investing is always have a core holding in fixed income.

John Bogle, founder of Vanguard, is 80 years old. He was recently on CNBC television and said he was 80% in fixed income and 20% in stocks. He lost only 10% in the recent meltdown of the market. This is probably a good ratio of stocks to bonds when approaching retirement.

Now we have the advent of the IRA - Individual Retirement Account. This bill was tagged onto another bill in Congress. The politicians never anticipated that this bill would actually spawn a huge market of mutual funds. They really believed that this tagged on IRA bill would never be used by many people. Politicians would be self serving by passing it and using it themselves. Surprise!

The investment business now really started to take off. There was a huge increase of growth in the financial markets. The best and brightest were entering the financial industry in record numbers. Math and science were no longer the big attraction for the young, it was business that commanded the largest number of bright young talent with the best salaries.

Also at this time the Japanese started to really kick our butt in the production of electronic equipment and began taking some of the prize real estate deals on the American soil. Rockefeller Center in New York City was purchased by Japanese backed investors and one Japanese politician commented "Americans study banking and Wall Street while we study science and math." The Nikkei hit 39,000 or so and then collapsed in 1989. It has never really come back. We are talking about a 20 year recession. They could have used some management because they took a bath on a 20 year depressed stock market.

The bottom line is that one should understand the journey or genealogy of the people that manage your money. One concept that I use is to invest in fixed income and only invest the dividends and interest from these in stocks. At the end of every year I collect all interest and dividends, pool them, and decide what to invest in for the next year. I do not reinvest any interest dividends except in tax free accounts.

In 1983 I made a good friend who had been a bond broker on Wall Street for 5 years. He taught me how to invest in bonds. I did well for the little money that I had. I wanted to invest in stocks, at least to nibble. This was a much harder task. I would buy the minimum amount of a mutual fund, watch it, read everything about funds that I could.

The problem was that the fund industry was growing at such an astounding rate that I couldn't keep up. The market dropped in October 1987. I waited until February or March and invested in two mutual funds with the help of a broker. I sold them about one or so years later and did fairly well, but not as well as the fund's advertisement claimed. It was at this point that I realized one must take all profit proceeds out of investments every year, pool them and check the actual results in dollars you collect. There are no lies here. I am presently hearing that some people that invested with Bernie Madoff are not as bad off as others. Some withdrew a percentage of principle on a monthly or quarterly basis. If they withdrew a percent of their principle and/or their interest dividends for the year, they actually may not have made out as badly. The other factor is taxes. I always used these yearly proceeds to pay additional taxes if need be. Now some people reinvest all dividend-interest income and those that did with Madoff paid taxes on bogus income that most certainly is irretrievable.

The next driving force of the economy that will come will have to come from science, technology, and or mathematics. In years past, manufacturing was the driving force of the engine of growth that propelled our economy and gave us the highest standard of living in the world. World class consumption of goods and services - conspicuous consumption - if you will, will not be enough to keep us as the number one economy in the world. In other words, the consumer and his or her credit card will not be enough to be an engine of growth. We must see a reversion to science, technology or mathematics to drive our economy in the future.

I applaud Phil Mickelson and his wife for their special foundation for encouraging students to study and excel in the subjects of science, math and technology. I have a younger friend who is a cofounder of a Power Engineering firm in Tennessee. He needed to hire two new Power Engineers. Being in the heart of the historical Tennessee Valley Authority he felt it would be no problem. He couldn't find qualified people. He ultimately hired one Engineer from India and one from China. This was additional work for him because he had to deal with green cards, work visas, etc. Wake up America.

We will have to see more of the best and brightest enter the science and math fields. (Remember, Engineering is math and science together and Computer Science is a subspecialty of Engineering.)

Chapter 4

In retrospect, when the brokerage houses and the banks merged (the birth of investment banks), concurrently we also were having rapid growth in the mutual fund industry. We now had a new breed of financiers called investment bankers that commanded huge salaries for their expertise. Prior to this, brokerage houses either had to earn their money from their own services or borrow money on the open market. But with the merger came new access to huge amounts of capital that was formerly held by the banks. These were now able to finance mergers and acquisitions and along came derivatives and other "financial instruments." Most investors did not understand all of this terminology and many of the professionals did not understand them either. I can remember one television interview with Alan Greenspan and he was trying to explain what a derivative was. I wasn't impressed.

Most investors were confused by the huge movement of money, investment banking, mergers and acquisitions, along with the legal fees involved. This led to an even more flight to mutual funds. This most could understand. One buys shares and the mutual fund company buys stocks. Simple enough. I stopped counting the total number of mutual funds when it reached 5,800.

The pundits were all over the television channels, newspapers, magazines, and internet telling which stocks to buy. We have traced professional business goals, MBA's, then investment banking, but have neglected to mention C.F.A.'s. These are Chartered Financial Analysts. These comprise about 70,000 people worldwide (at my last count several years ago). Most likely you have never met one. We all know what a Certified Financial Planner is. A Chartered Financial Analyst is to a Certified Financial Planner what a C.P.A. is to an accountant. The CFA's have a strong background in mathematics, read and interpret the long spreadsheets to determine credit worthiness, financial stability, and growth potential of a company. To obtain a C.F.A., you usually need an MBA, and have passed a yearly exam for 3 years (obviously Part I, Part II and Part III.) These are the people that do the research as to what stocks to buy. Most of the guests you see on television either employ or pay for the service of CFA's; they do not research themselves. This is hard and tedious work and rather time consuming.

When Harry Markopoulos was asked to determine what was going on with Bernie Madoff it took him less than 15 minutes to determine some fraud was evident, but he didn't know if it was insider trading or a Ponzi scheme. It took him 4 hours to prove that Madoff's stock picking mathematically was impossible (2) I don't know if Markopoulos is a CFA, but he has a huge background in mathematics.

So you have an evolution of money managers in the early days which were totally unregulated to a point where there are certified people smarter than the regulators. The Securities and Exchange Commission totally ignored the 5 alerts that Markopoulos sent to them. (2) By the way, I believe Bernie Madoff's fund was an unregistered fund. By understanding this genealogy of money management it accentuates some of the pitfalls.

I always think of a boxing champion. When he walks up the 7 steps into the boxing ring to defend his title, no one really knows how much his last fight took out of him. I think of the United States as the economic champion and no one knows which untoward financial event will lead to the downfall of our nation as the economic leader of the world. The housing crisis with its widespread global effects was of internal origin that could have crushed our banking system as well as our financial system. Our failure may very well come from within, not from an external terrorist plot.

With all of the financial professionals that were directly or indirectly involved with Bernie Madoff, including those involved with feeder funds, very few could figure out his fraud. Some of these "feeders" were collecting hundreds of millions of dollars in fees and didn't figure out fraud? Well this is what I think of when the television pundits say, if CEO's aren't paid ridiculously high salaries we will lose that talent. What talent? I could lose that huge amount of company stock value and work for ½ of these large salaries and so could you.

Hey, you know what. In England CEO's earn about 40 times what the average employee earns. In Japan it is 30 or so times. Europe is somewhere in the middle. In the United States, it is 400 times on average of what the typical worker earns. That's all you hear from the television pundits is that we will lose the talent. But they all say we are in a global economy with international companies, free markets, etc., etc. So why don't we really do what management has done to the working class in the United States and shop globally for a CEO. We could offer them 60 times what an average worker earns and they would be thrilled. Perhaps there would be something left over for the shareholders. Ah yes, the fickle finger of fate.

"So goes General Motors, so goes the United States." You remember that quote, it wasn't that long ago. I was close to GM workers in the 1970's and was able to attend some GM open houses in the Tarrytown, New York plant. It was not an uncommon occurrence to see a Japanese auto employee with a clipboard taking notes at the assembly line of GM. I am sure they learned something from some free observations. All during the GM hearings no one suggested for GM to duplicate the management of say Toyota, Honda or Nissan. We could have duplicated the number, salaries and duties of the management. Then let the GM workers do their thing. It would end the finger pointing between management, labor unions and politicians. We would start to see if and where the talent lies. What I really do fear is "so goes GM, so goes the United States."

(2) CNBC - David Faber's documentary entitled "The House of Cards"

Chapter 5

Fortunately we have some smart people like Harry Markopoulos with a great sense of civic duty who attempted to correct an egregious situation and stand up for the shareholders. It seems that the Securities and Exchange Commission did not listen and were not able to decipher the problem even though it was spoon fed to them. So one cannot rely on the government to protect your assets. With some of the smartest people now present in financial endeavors, we have introduced new terms such as financial engineering. We also have derivatives, naked shorts, etc., etc. etc. In order to combat some of these complex issues like Collaterized Debt Obligations I swap some of my money from stocks over into fixed safe securities. In other words one has taken only the interest and/or proceeds from your initial investment in fixed income. One has invested the proceeds only in mutual stock funds or ETF's and as the funds hopefully grow, slide a portion of that growth back into fixed income on a systematic basis. The temptation is to let the good times roll. The hard part is to save the initial seed money in the beginning. Once you can master living below your means you can get the system working for you and not fear financial destruction. I have invested in mutual funds, index mutual funds, exchange traded funds and a smaller number of individual stocks. When you have a stock that doubles, always sell ½ of it - that way you are working on their money. It is so tempting to let it roll. I did once and I got burned. Put the profit in fixed income.

What does all this mean to you?? It means that saving is a cultural thing. It is a way of life. Does it mean that you have to be cheap? No, it means you have to be smart. You very well may be smarter than the people that are managing your money. "Power to the People"!!! When you pay huge credit card fees, you are working for the man. You want to have your money working for you; that is the bottom line. We have been accustomed to just borrow when we have a life's need. No one calls you cheap when you can pay for long term care insurance for your elder years or if you pay for a loved one's bone marrow transplant to save their (or your) life. They call you smart.

The second point is that business schools have several ways to teach their students how to manage a business. Many of them do a very fine job . The creativity to start a world class business that will drive the engine of growth for America will have to come from math, science and technology. I am talking about companies like Apple, Google, IBM, Microsoft, and the medical technology companies which are too numerous to mention. Business schools can only manage the business aspect of these companies and don't confuse financial engineering (with its financial instruments) with real engineering.

Chapter 6

"Free Market Capitalism is the Best Pathway to Prosperity" -- Larry Kudlow. (1)

I have a hard time getting my arms around this. I believe it, but in light of recent events I question whether we actually go there.

Free market capitalism is basically survival of the fittest. My interpretation would be "let each become all he or she is capable of being regardless of race, color, creed or national origin." One would rise or fall on their own abilities. We could all remember the games we used to play as children, in the days before electronic games. I guess I am really dating myself here. You remember a group of kids would make up the rules for a game (not very different than many of the concepts used in MBA schools as group training). Back to the kids, the games would begin and there was one kid that would always want to change the rules when he or she began to lose. This is what I sometimes see in the financial banking system. Let the good times roll, big salaries, private jets, huge expense accounts. The financial hierarchy wants borderless commerce throughout North America, free trade outsourcing to the lowest bidder no matter what the cost, as long as it can be done cheaper. Little or no regulation, don't even enforce port or border laws. They had it all their way and the profits were rolling in. Then we had the devastation of 2008, 40% - 50% in the stock market. But wait, we don't want the downside to free market capitalism, we want only the upside. Somewhat like the child that wants to change the rules when he starts to lose. This is totally against free market capitalism. Now when things are going bad due to their own poor management they want a government bailout. Once you or your organization takes the first dollar of government money for any type of bailout, all capitalism is off the table. You are a government employee whether you like it or not. There are no private jets, no big company expense accounts, no big bonuses. Your salary is a matter of public record. You are now a government employee, you are now either completely unemployed or part of a socialistic system. What part of this can't people understand? As the geniuses (talent) keep managing, we drift closer and closer to European socialism.

Now comes the hardest part. As Shakespeare said, "Know thyself." This applies nowhere more than investing in any form of stocks. Know thy own risk tolerance. I always like to move in a forward direction, sometimes in a little forward direction and in a bad market staying even is okay. But I am a real poor loser in the market. I have worked for my money, paid taxes and what I have left, after expenses, I invest. I don't like to lose. Each of us has our own view of money which predicates our risk tolerance. You can't be wrong on this, you really have to know thyself. If I take risk with my money, I like it to be with interest from fixed income, not the seed or core money that I have worked for. I feel that if you invest in stock in a company you should at least get some dividends just for respect. This is more of my personal philosophy but one has to develop one's own view and method. Peter Lynch always said invest in what you know, and we all know about various things we use in daily life, hobbies we have, work that we do. After reading and studying and viewing all financial news I could find, Forbes magazine listed Lindner Dividend as their number one fund several years in a row in the early 1990's. It was originally formed by Mr. Lindner and was then run by his capable protégé Eric Ryback. This fund invested in solid companies that paid dividends and would be considered somewhat blue chip lower risk companies. I bought this fund after multiple attempts of investing the minimum amount (usually $1000) in various other funds with little or no success. Lindner Dividend seemed to fit my philosophy well and looked to be a winner. Then the market trend changed. The fashion of the industry changed. The big thing then became buyback of stocks, and merger and acquisitions abounded. The problem became that fewer and fewer stocks were paying dividends. Many of the stocks that continued to pay dividends were dropping in stock value. I sold my shares, lost some money, but with the dividends I collected over several years I only lost $100. Another lesson here: Dividend-paying stocks provide a buffer to loss.

Now I had to find another fund. It took several years to really find that second fund that I was comfortable with. After constant reading I came across Dodge & Cox Balanced Fund. This was really hard to find because this fund company does not advertise at all. In 1994 Dodge & Cox had only a stock fund, a bond fund, and a balanced fund which was a combo of the two. This company was started in the early 1930's right in the heart of the depression. No problem finding a track record here. It was managed by a team that consisted of mostly Harvard and Stanford graduates. The turnover rate was about 20%, the operating costs were low, no money was wasted on advertisement. The company used sound research and preferred to keep stock three to five years. I put our IRA's in all three funds and purchased the balanced and new international fund outside our IRA's. Many years the balanced fund (with bonds) beat the S&P 500 stock index. I held these funds for fourteen years and then sold. I also had bought another dividend paying fund with a great track record called T.Rowe Price Equity Income run by Brian Rogers. I held this fund for thirteen years and also sold out at the same time I sold Dodge & Cox balanced and our IRA's. It was the summer of 2008 and the time was right to get out of stocks.

(1) Daily on CNBC television show "Kudlow and Company."

Chapter 7

Ah yes, when to sell, that is the really big problem! You can buy at any spot on the way up but when to sell is a real problem. Trigger, not Roy Rogers' horse but a red flag alert, I call them triggers. These alert one to really pay attention that any downturn is more than a bump in the road. I met a businessman in 2004 or 2005, this was about the time the McMansions were abounding in our middle class neighborhood, and I had said to my wife that the salaries in our area did not merit this high end housing. This was simple observation. I used to run into this businessman about every week or so and we would stop and chat for ½ to one hour about various topics. I asked him about his son and how his son was doing. I knew he was very proud of his son and he began to tell me about his son's recent success. Many times it pays to be a good listener. My friend relates his story. His son was working as a teller in one of the local regional banks. I had had an account in this bank several years before and, believe me, this bank was really small potatoes. Anyway, the bank manager comes up to his son, the teller, and tells him that the bank needs someone to be a risk manager and his son is it. He is to read this book, which the manager gives him, and then he becomes the bank's official risk manager. "That's it?" I questioned. "That's all there was to it," my friend replies. Well anyway, this small bank merges with another small bank. These two banks merge again before they are bought again by a large institution, all within a few years, all of which was common knowledge in the community. My friend tells me his son is earning $250,000 per year as a risk manager but is worth $500,000 per year. He is going to only interview at the higher salary level. He feels that his present company or a new one will match that salary. I meet his son and he really is only in his 30's. This was a quick rise to almost instant success, so in my mind I am relating all these houses, loans and mortgages to these local banks and risk. I have a friend who has been in banking (commercial loans) for 35 years and I asked what risk management was and had him explain it to me just for the record. No surprises here, it's the risk that banks take with their loans and investments. This has got me on alert. How could you read a book and become an expert in such a short time. Sometimes there is so much information around you and knowledgeable people are willing to share it. Definitely a trigger here.

I like mutual funds that do not have more than 100 stocks but have at least 30 stocks. I always read the quarterly reports including stocks bought and stocks sold. I have not second guessed any of the trades of Dodge & Cox until the summer report of 2008. As I read the report I noticed that they purchased Ford & GM to the tune of almost 3% of the fund in each company. Now this was my alert. This was definitely not to my liking and a sure trigger to sell. I stomped around the house and mumbled for 24 hours. I then sold all of our Dodge & Cox IRA's and the balanced fund outside of our IRA's. I also sold my T.Rowe Price Equity income. A couple months later everything came apart.

You see we all know about things like I said before -- from work, hobbies, family and friends. I love old cars, not the expensive cars, but Fords, Chevys and Plymouths. I love those old flathead engines. When you attempt to start these cars, with their 6 volt starters, they cough and burp and sound like it's the end of their life. Then all of a sudden, voila, they spring to life. I live in a world of distributors with contact points and condensers, 6 volt electrical systems, carburetors instead of fuel injection, generators instead of alternators. Some have positive ground systems instead of the modern 12 volt negative ground system that is used today. I love it when the old flathead engines kick to life and then you adjust the manual choke to smooth out the running engine. An odd combination, these depression era cars and an intense interest in economics, or is it???

After many years of intense reading on car repairs and attending night classes on the same at the local high school, I was able to tune up my daily drivers and save a lot of money, but more important have a lot of fun "doing it myself." I have owned Fords, Chevys and Plymouths (Chrysler products). I spent many hours under the hood and under the bodies working on these cars, especially doing my own work.

For daily driving I, like so many other Americans, have drifted toward Japanese cars for their durability and reliability. All of the modern cars need less and less maintenance and they all depend on computer diagnosis. That is why I always keep at least one old car to tinker with. It's my mental therapy.

What I concluded from all of this experience was that G.M., Ford, and Chrysler were going to be in big trouble, especially when in competition with some of the Japanese automakers. The second thing I realized was that Dodge & Cox really was at a loss as to what to buy in the stock market. The third thing I became aware of was that the Dodge & Cox company was owned privately outside of the public stock market, and these people probably drove BMW's, Mercedes and/or Lexus and certainly did not lie under their cars and do any of their own work.

I immediately called the five people that I suggested invest in Dodge & Cox and told them that I was selling out. I believe it is an excellent investment company and still kept my international stock that was outside of my IRA.

Chapter 8

There were a minority of investors that actually saw a serious problem in our financial sector and predicted an imminent disaster. To me, it was as clear as daylight. What I can't, for the life of me, figure out is how no one in power in these brokerage houses or banks or insurance companies like A.I.G. could not visualize and act to prevent such a financial disaster for their company. Some call us right brained, odd ball theory promoters, believers in new or different combination factors. Some critics are not so kind. I look at it as light hitting a prism with the light rays being reflected at different angles. We all view a prism at different angles and see different rays reflected. These may be developed or inherited. What I do know is that it isn't over yet; not by a long shot. There are serious issues that are long term problems with long term solutions. The stock market will fluctuate but we have many serious issues to resolve. The way we approach problems and the way we see them are a unique form of intelligence that needs more explanation. When a basketball player views the basket and his brain computes the distance to the basket, the neuromuscular function is able to translate this to a physical motion; it is an immeasurable form of intelligence.

Andrew Tanzer in his excellent article about "What went wrong with Dodge & Cox," Kiplinger 2/2009, says and I quote, "Still, Dodge & Cox could benefit from adding some intuitive, right brained types to a staff replete with left brained Stanford & Harvard graduates. That might help the firm anticipate the next 100 year storm before it hits." Tanzer also agrees that Dodge & Cox is a quality company with an excellent long term record and are excellent choices for long term investors. There were numerous others that warned of failure in our financial system, but they definitely were few and far between. It doesn't matter how one arrives at the correct end result as long as one gets there in time.

I personally believe that for myself, it was all of those long afternoons in college labs where we repeated laboratory experiments, some of which we knew what the result would be and some of which we had no idea what the end result would be. I think that people with science and/or math backgrounds develop certain deductive reasoning that derives its base from laboratory experimental techniques. I would say this would be my right brained approach to the problem.

Meredith Whitney called the housing bubble, when she was working for Oppenheimer, I believe. She has since been able to start her own firm. Another good source of information is David Walker of the Peterson Group.

Nouriel Roubini of New York University and John Makin of the American Enterprise Institute warned that the excessive leveraging and poor lending practices that abounded were going to lead to financial problems. There most definitely are others that warned of shaky derivative practices, poor lending practices, over borrowing, etc.,etc.,etc. Some involved the housing market, some lending by banks, some poor, poor management decisions by brokerage houses. My favorite one of all is Kyle Bass (see David Faber's House of Cards) and the hedge fund he operates out of Dallas Texas. He traveled to New York City and met and gave a presentation to one of the brokerage houses on the precarious state of the housing market in this country. They pretty well blew him off. He then purchased credit default swaps, essentially bet that the brokerages were going to lose money on the mortgages that they loaned money for. The last count I heard was that he earned 600% in 18 months on those credit default swaps. (2)

My question is, where are the bonus babies, you know the ones that worked for various firms that took bailout funds from the federal government and obviously from the taxpayer. Where was all of that talent that wants hundreds of thousands of dollars in bonus money because they have talent; why couldn't any of them see or call the oncoming train? From everything I could find, all of the warnings came from individuals or smaller institutions run by such individuals. If there was so much talent in the TARP (federal program subsidized by the taxpayers to bail out big banks), why did the banks not see the problem as others did??

Some people compensated for their pain by saying they sold their stocks before the 50% correction. Some went on to say that they were so devastated by the financial loss, in some cases 50% of their portfolio, that they could not face the reality of it. The only way they had to deal with it was complete denial, and they really believed they sold.

Well, I can tell you that I sold 90% of all my stocks prior to the meltdown and if I can beat the "HOT SHOTS" so can you. I have told you about triggers, they are things that you know. There are also people that I follow, and I will give you the names of such. Some have websites for free - Peter Schiff (just go under Euro-Pacific Investments) many good articles on political economics, he even sorts out the articles and they are not lengthy at all; Meredith Whitney (she has her own company now); David Tice (Prudent Bear Fund); FPA funds Bob Rodriguez and Steve Romick; John Makin of the American Enterprise Institute; Nouriel Roubini (New York University); Bill Fleckenstein, and Jim Rogers for commodities. Do not forget to add Professor Ravi Batra and don't forget Robert Shiller who wrote "Irrational Exuberance". There are others, and as you read some of the above they may cross reference other good names. It is a lengthy list, but most are somewhat specialized and you may read a certain person for banking, brokerages, another for banks, another for housing, etc.,etc. After a while you can get great info just off their websites and add names of your own. Soon you will have developed your own philosophy and you can spot and pick your topics related to a person. Sometimes some may seem too negative, but they will bring most of what you hear on television to a middle ground reality.

(2) CNBC David Faber's documentary entitled "The House of Cards"

Chapter 9

We have a huge amount of debt to pay off from the housing bubble. The powers that be are trying to bag it, wrap it, can it, in order to make it disappear. They can use smoke and mirrors, the peanut shell trick, slap lipstick on it and try to sweep it under the rug, but they just can't make it go away. It has to work its way through the system and it is ugly. There are too many people that are upside down in their houses. In other words, they owe more on the house than it is worth.

I always felt that Alan Greenspan waited too long and then tightened credit at least three times too many after his famous 1996 statement about "irrational exuberance". Hey, I loved it, I was still buying bonds during the tech bubble and the interest was good. When the tech bubble burst, I knew it was going to drive the economy down harder than if he didn't make the last three raises in interest rates. The Fed was trying to stem the tech bubble which I don't think was their primary mission. So at this point, the economy needed a boost after the tech bubble burst. Then the Fed adopted a different attitude and lowered rates, especially after 9/11/01. The terrorists caused a stay at home attitude after 9/11/01, the economy really needed help and there was no encouragement for saving, especially with a dropping interest environment. Everyone seemed to be frozen in place. Americans needed to start spending. Sharp cuts in interest rates were in order and implemented.

President Bush went on television in 2002 and said, and I quote, "too many families, minorities, do not own a home." In 2004 Greenspan said on television that he wanted more loans and I quote, "we need new kinds of loans, new product alternatives to consumer loans."

During all of this, the standards for home lending were set by the government agencies of Fannie Mae and Freddie Mac. Then these government agencies were wrought with accounting scandals. There was a turnover of top management and the business focus was in disarray. This left the door open for a new business model that was less structured than Fannie & Freddie and open to what President Bush and Alan Greenspan wanted.

At this point I must refer to the excellent documentary by David Faber called "The House of Cards" on CNBC television. (2) This is the best program that I have seen and kudos to David Faber for his excellent work. I recommend that everyone watch it on CNBC, view it twice. It explains how the collapse of the housing market really happened. Faber points out how mortgage originators met an unregulated Wall Street and Faber does an interesting interview with Alan Greenspan. Greenspan says that he was unaware that there were so many sub prime mortgages in the system until it was brought to his attention by one of his assistants. Greenspan says that many of the brightest executives were aware of the problem but thought they could get out in time. Greenspan felt that "the best and brightest failed us." Faber's interview with Kyle Bass produces a different picture. When Bass interviews one of the big brokerage houses that was underwriting these loans, he found a few young guys, a couple of years out of business school, without any experience in a down market. He reviews their program model and finds that their model is based on the premise that housing prices will never go down. (2) Wait a minute, these are the best and brightest? I am having a flashback here to my first year in college where my roommate couldn't perform in science and math and was railroaded into a business program. I know I couldn't be correct all these years. Times must have changed. This program model was the risk management benchmark for this huge brokerage firm that was doing a great deal of sub prime lending. So my friend, whose son was a teller that became a risk manager after reading one book, was right on target.

Faber also does an interview with a Ms. Rutledge, who is very forthcoming with information on the rating agency that she worked for. In this interview she frankly admits that she was unsophisticated as a rater of these debt obligations and it was relatively easy to change the rating on an obligation from BBB to Triple A. As far as credit worthiness goes, it was easy to raise the rating of sub prime mortgages to Triple A. "Garbage in, garbage out" was the phrase used in the interview. (2)

Now supervising all of this neglect were executives and consultants earning tens of millions of dollars per year. We know we had them in many of the TARP bailed out banks.

Now if you add up the annual salaries from 2001 to August 2008, some of these bank managers' compensations totaled in the hundreds of millions of dollars. Under the guidance of this "talent," debt was wrapped, canned and bagged and sold as quality securities. Fifty percent was sold overseas. Trillions of dollars of wealth evaporated when the mortgagees could not pay their debts. Do you think our foreign neighbors are going to be so eager to buy our debt again? Our multimillionaire bankers kept all of their money that had been derived as commissions from transacting the sale of sub-prime mortgages. I am sure very little, if any, will be recovered from the executives that led their companies down the road of destruction. How can one perform so badly and have the audacity to keep tens of millions of dollars? What arrogance we Americans have. These people came very close to breaking our financial system and I believe we were just days away from financial collapse. We have crossed from the military industrial complex that ran the Vietnam War to the military industrial financial complex of today. We have become two economies in America today. One economy is that of Main Street and the second is the financial bubble of Wall Street. It is the financial bubble that almost cost us economic collapse. They confuse greed and arrogance with talent. The layer we have peeled back at this point highlights the greed of the hundred-million-dollar executives of the past decade, but lying just one layer below is another strata of executives who have followed the same practices and whose compensations fall in the range of tens of millions of dollars -- sums that are deemed too small to investigate and expose. The investment banks feel real flush with so much talent that they are still giving huge bonuses and can't circumnavigate the greed part. They really believe they should be granted huge bonuses because they have been anointed by the "divine right of kings." They fail to realize that a twelfth grader can borrow money from the Fed at almost zero percent and loan it out at almost five percent and make money. The television shows need not worry about Wall Street losing talent; they just have to peel back the top layer of greed and arrogance and it will reveal another layer that will do it all over again. President Obama sees this and they say he is anti Wall Street.

There is an old embryological theorem that says "ontogeny recapitulates phylogeny." This basically says that the embryo from fertilization to birth mimics all of the struggles of man from the beginning to the present. You may ask, what the hell does that mean? It means unless you curb their power, the next layer of "talent" will do it all again, but this next time we really don't know how much that fight will take out of the champion.

The positive aspect of all of this is that probably the Dow 30 will be the poster child of our economy and the industrial military financial complex will do everything possible to shore up its (and a few other companies) viability. Does "too big to fail" ring a bell? Besides these are international companies and may have more potential for growth. You will have to pay attention carefully as to where to buy in, if at all.

(2) CNBC David Faber's documentary entitled "The House of Cards"

Chapter 10

We have not really addressed the credit card crisis. Some credit card issuers have already started to lower the borrowing limits on some individuals with a variety of cute tricks. The bottom line is that we have a credit card industry that is running scared. This could be the next bubble ready to pop and the issuers realize that they have overextended credit to many who may very well be sub prime borrowers. Many people were refinancing their home mortgages, based on the premise that home prices would always rise, and using any cash taken out of the transaction to pay off any credit card debt incurred over the past year. This was done on a repetitive basis and it worked for years as long as home prices escalated. With home prices plummeting, many people are upside down in their homes and have overextended their credit cards. Gone is the option to refinance a mortgage and take cash out of this refinancing to pay off credit card debt.

We can't continue to export debt as a national product. How long will other countries continue to support our financial bubble with our huge bonuses and purchase that financial "product" that will turn worthless. David Faber showcases a town called Narvik, Norway in his documentary. (2) The Town Council places 25% of their budget in C.D.O.'s that were supposedly Triple A rated. There were also seven other towns in Norway that invested in similar products. Narvik's investment turned worthless and was "manufactured" by Wall Street. Some "manufacturing" product we produced. Now do you think these towns will come back to the marketplace and buy more? I don't think so!! We have individuals who are in debt and we have a government from local to state to federal that is in huge debt. What makes us so arrogant to think that other people from other countries should finance what we cannot afford??

David Faber, again in the same program, highlights several people in the chain of C.D.O.'s that were Triple A rated but were really sub prime. (2) The interesting interviews yielded a tremendous insight into the schematics of the housing crisis. The point that glared at me was that when asked, no one accepted guilt or responsibility for the pain and anguish that resulted. They all kept their piece of the action and moved on without guilt or remorse. One lost his job with a big unnamed investment firm and set up his own "consulting" business. Another left Bear Stearns a few weeks before its collapse. There is a long lineage of bad debt that may have started with the original mortgage application, through the mortgage originator, through unregulated Wall Street, through the rating agencies, out into a financial "product" that really was garbage. We have credit card debt that I hope is not securitized the same way as mortgages. We cannot survive that. But isn't it wonderful that no one was at fault and all were able to keep the profits they reaped.

During this documentary Faber also does an interview with IRA Wagoner, one of the financial engineers, formerly of Bear Stearns. (2) Faber's question was that if there is a possible future money stream, one could almost securitize anything? Wagoner's answer was," You could certainly look at it." This answer is what really bothers me. These financial products could be rewrapped and also sold as debt certificates laced with sub prime borrowers that are unable to meet their payments. Hey, what about student loans, we could securitize that debt and sell it. Also there is commercial credit and commercial real estate that also could be securitized. Is this what becomes of our financial products? This is what we sell? When Faber asks the Mayor of Narvik what she learned after all of this her answer was, "Don't believe nice men in Armani suits." (2) I guess that says it all.

(2) CNBC David Faber's documentary entitled "The House of Cards"

Chapter 11

Whatever happened to Rooster Jones?

The time was the early 1980's and I was in New York at the time and had the opportunity on a beautiful Fall Saturday afternoon to attend an Army football game. A friend purchased the tickets for me so how could I refuse. Army was playing Pitt who had an outstanding young quarterback named Dan Marino.

Wanda, the wife, and I packed a picnic basket and really had a nice afternoon. What I learned from other tailgating fans that afternoon was that Army football players really had limited time to spend on practicing football because of their rigorous academic programs. It seems from the information that I received, the teams that Army played were able to devote considerably more time to football practice and Army was always at a disadvantage when they played big name teams. It was a great football game. Although Army played well, Pitt was the dominant team that day. But the thing that I remembered most was the choreography between Dan Marino and one of his receivers named Rooster Jones. Any viewer could tell that many hours of practice between the two had transpired to produce such a beautiful result. Dan Marino would drop back to pass and Rooster Jones would race down field making a quick break and then circled to confuse the Army defensive backs. Dan Marino would throw the ball high and far to a spot on the field where there were no players of either team. Surely, this pass would wind up in the dirt as an incomplete pass. Lo and behold, along comes Rooster Jones and at the pinnacle of his jump, the juxtaposition of the ball, and Rooster's receptive hands is as well choreographed as any ballet. It truly was a thing of beauty to watch. Now, mind you, Rooster was an average sized guy, but very fast.

I always wondered what happened to Rooster Jones. Dan Marino went on to play for the Miami Dolphins and had a stellar career which will definitely springboard him to the Football Hall of Fame. At Miami he threw to two great receivers named Clayton and Duper. I never did find out whatever happened to Rooster Jones. Perhaps he did sign a contract with a professional team, but I can't ever recall hearing or reading his name in the professional ranks.

Returning home that afternoon I was thinking about how the industrial military complex that ran the Vietnam War had become the industrial military educational complex. As you remember I earlier added the word financial to this dictum. Educational and financial are not mutually exclusive. Filling the football and other college sports arenas is a very big attribute for the financial success of colleges.

At what price do we fill these arenas? The answer is at any price. Generate money, that is the basis of the free market capitalism that we aspire to. Colleges pay some of their coaches more than world class professors. Some college presidents must know, in their hearts, that they don't have to charge the tuition that they do. Granted, some of the big endowments of universities may have suffered in the stock market downturn of 2008, but from a prestige point of view, some chancellors must feel that if they do not keep up with the escalating cost of tuition, this could send a message that somehow their school is inferior.

Thomas G. Donlon writes an interesting article in the editorial commentary of "*Barron's*," July 27, 2009. It's title is, "The Best of our Energies and Skills." He commemorates the 40th anniversary of the U.S. astronauts landing on the moon. He says how little has been done for the last 30 plus years (since 1970) in advancing the space program and that could be the reason that we, as a country, have not been doing very well. Earlier I stated that after we put a man on the moon, we avenged Sputnik and our focus changed. Our focus changed away from math and science. About this time and shortly after, colleges became big business. There was money to be made and a product to sell. What they sold were packages. I would say in the early 1980's, packages were starting to become popular. Before this, student loans were popular, but limited in size and used to supplement somewhat more reasonable college costs.

As the stock market started to take off, so did college costs; they seemed to run parallel in theme. Again the focus was away from science and math into many new areas with study and living abroad programs. Concurrently, the cost of skyrocketing college degrees necessitated debt packages to cover these high costs.

Now students and parents had to file lengthy applications with financial verification in order to obtain the best package for the student. In other words, weigh the best debt level package against the best school that is affordable. Many sleepless nights were spent by student and parent alike. Again, we are selling and packaging debt against the thought of one's child being a total failure. The parents become neurotic, the students cannot just focus on studies with their heavy burden of debt, and each year the cost escalates by huge percentages. I think you have the picture here. We are selling more debt. But remember there is good and bad debt, with educational costs being good debt, so we are told.

I attended a seminar about 10 years ago and saw a familiar name of a professor I had in graduate school many years before on the program. This professor had just finished his graduate program and it was his first or second year of teaching when I was halfway through my graduate program. Some people you remember because they are remarkably good. This was certainly an unexpected pleasant surprise to what I thought might be a boring day. His lecture was about 1 ½ hours and believe me he was as good as ever. He didn't lose a step. After the lecture I introduced myself and we exchanged pleasantries. I asked him why I don't see him on the lecture circuit. He says that he has moved on to a new university since I had first met him, and his job now is completely fund raising. This lecture was just an anomaly for him. I thought to myself this was a real shame because he should be working with students and research.

Chapter 12

On a different note, some of the college degree programs are not worth the cost. Some of these $40,000 to $50,000 per year programs are not going to qualify students for jobs that pay enough for students to honor their debt obligations. Yes, does it remind you of the McMansions and the salaries needed to support them that I mentioned earlier? Well take this to the bank. Colleges and Universities have expanded their programs to include degrees from which students can't get jobs or if they can, they will be underpaid. This means that Sallie Mae, I believe it's now called SLR, will be under pressure to collect their loans and there will be defaults. Sallie Mae, bank loans and colleges are all tied to these high level debt packages that students now carry. SLR must have smelled a problem because there are a few nuances whereby you can reduce or eliminate student loans. One is if you work for the government for ten years and there are other reductions that will be forthcoming.

I have a friend that I have known for a long time and he is a well respected PhD in Psychology. In a casual conversation one day, he revealed that this was a second career. He had previously attained a PhD in French Renaissance literature and could not find employment in anything that resembled work close to his field. He did state that at the time college costs were low compared to today so, although he lost time in preparing for his present career, it did not cost him much money. Not so today! I know another PhD in history that went on to obtain another degree in a more employable industry for the same reason.

First I did some research on a local two year technical college and obtained a list of degree programs. They included computer technology, civil engineering, paralegal studies, culinary arts, green building construction, advanced healthcare case management, etc. All in all, not too bad a selection to keep the cost reward ratio pretty good, but make sure these credits are transferable to a four year school.

Then I started to look at four year programs out of the area and more on a national scale. I found many of the four-year degrees at $40,000 to $50,000 per year were in areas like history, communications, political science, liberal arts, etc. I called up a friend, who is a high school administrator, and asked him if there were any teaching jobs in these related fields. He told me that he had one history teaching position recently and had 150 applications for that one position. Parents are so afraid for their children's futures that they will mortgage a debt package out for 30 years. I know that you have a hard time believing this, but it's true.

I guess weddings are a great place for congregation and information. Kyle Bass met his most important contact at a wedding in the south of Spain. (2) This was the encounter that directed his plan to short the housing market by purchasing credit default swaps from some of the larger investment brokerage houses. My encounter was not as intriguing.

Wanda, the wife, and I are sitting at a wedding reception in the New York area with several other couples. Seated were a dentist and his wife, a recently graduated dentist and his wife and a recently graduated M.D. and her husband. Somehow the cost of present day education came up and I had the benefit of a two generation perspective since the dentists were decades apart in age.

During the 1960's a federal government announcement suggested there would be a shortage of dentists and physicians in the future assuming that population growth remained at a constant rate. This was not a bad idea and probably fairly accurate in its conclusion. Not being in the business of medical education, the federal government decided to endow money to medical and dental schools that would expand their classes. Seems reasonable, and in 1965 some of the schools expanded with as little as four or five students. Most of the medical schools and all but one of the dental schools (in the state of Oregon I believe) participated in the program. Well you know us, if a little is good, more is always better.

All of the dental schools that I could find were affiliated with medical schools and for good reason. The basic medical core courses are pretty much the same for the first two years with the medical students going to the hospital for their second two years and the dental students going to the dental clinic for their second two years. This lends itself to a lot of sharing of lecture halls, laboratories, and many professors, with the dental schools not having to establish stand alone medical programs. Dollars saved through curriculum sharing.

Now there was one little caveat that the government did not realize. Most of the staffing in the dental clinic, which comprised the last two years of dental education, was composed of part time dentists. Now these part time dentists were practicing dentists that usually taught on the dental clinic "floor" from anywhere from one half day to usually a day and a half per week. The rest of the time they usually worked in their own offices. The fee basis on which the part time dentists were paid was minimal at best. They did it for a variety of reasons. Some liked the students and the camaraderie of fellow colleagues. Some liked the benefit of taking advanced courses tuition free. Others liked the prestige of saying that they taught dentistry at a university. Any of the above combinations was acceptable.

So this was also a cost saving move on the part of dental schools. Sharing the basic medical courses with the medical schools and operating the second two years of the dental education with a couple, or three, full time professors in each department, and the rest of the staff as low paid part timers. Root canal or crown & bridge would each have two or three full time professors and the rest of the clinic staff would be part timers staggered throughout the week. So would be the structure for all specialties in dentistry. The students loved it because they were actually working with every day practitioners that were performing in their offices the same procedures the students were studying. A win-win situation for everyone. During the 1960's the cost of dental education was modest, even though it usually followed a four year college degree. All things were rosy, at least for a while.

During the 1970's the federal government really kicked it up a notch and started to heavily fund these programs. With increased funding came increased control. Gradually the government wanted the dental schools to increase the number of full time teachers in the dental clinic and decrease the number of part time teachers. With this came increases in salaries and they now had to include other employment benefits. Everything seemed all right as long as the federal government continued to pour money into the dental schools. Then the obvious happened, the federal government decided that there was no longer a shortage of dentists and they discontinued all funding. A few schools closed, some used the reason that student quality was at fault, others became state affiliated for financial reasons. The bottom line was that the cost of dental education skyrocketed. There are six or eight non state affiliated dental schools at present and some of these can cost approximately $80,000 a year. Now this does not include the four years of college prior to dental school.

Now back to the wedding. The people seated at my table are telling me that some dental and medical students leave school with debt of $250,000 to $300,000. (Not hard to understand.) This takes a lot of creative financing with debt extended out to 30 years. You may say that these graduates may earn a lot of money, but none has specialized yet and to purchase or set up a dental practice can easily cost a couple of hundred thousand dollars. There are all kinds of enslavement.

Admittedly, I have chosen the extreme in selecting an M.D. and a D.D.S. as examples, but you can see how it can be applied to lesser economies of scale. We have now reached the industrial-military-financial-educational complex whereby the schools, along with banks and the federal government can cause financial enslavement of students. Somewhere there is a breaking point and parents will be hard pressed to help children pay back these loans when the parents can no longer use the equity in their houses and students have $50,000-a-year, four-year college debt. If after four years of a private college you are waiting tables or flipping burgers you are not going to pay back student loans. These student loans are in great jeopardy of defaulting.

I mention all of this because it is a travesty and will soon reach a breaking point. The other reason is that some way a financial engineer will restructure this debt, wrap it, can it, bag it, paint lipstick on it, get it rated triple A and call it a structured product. Don't purchase it! Financial engineering is not dead, it will resurface because much of the same high priced "talent" is still around; it has not been expunged from the system.

Many parents feel that the middle class lifestyle may be slipping away from future generations. The concept of each generation having a lifestyle better than the previous one is no longer a guarantee. We, as a country, have mortgaged the next generation with a heavy burden of debt. No longer can a person work for a company for their whole career, buy a house, have a family, and lead a comfortable lifestyle including a comfortable retirement, with a single non-college degree breadwinner. Times have changed drastically. Parents of children know this but haven't been able to cope with the high cost of private colleges. State colleges, with their reduced costs, offer an alternative but can still be costly.

This leaves the door open, and both the parents and students are vulnerable to extensive debt accumulation. One of the classic college moves is to give a student a great package the first year and a dwindling package each of the second, third and fourth years. The student can still keep up excellent grades, but the excuse that there are less funds available is the standard answer. In a private school, this can really run up the debt. Choose your curriculum well, research the job opportunities before you start a program. Be careful of your risk/reward ratio and watch out for sneaky debt. Some colleges will sell you a program that will be outdated by the time you finish the program. Colleges sell a product, they finance debt, and foster the fears of parents and students alike. If entering a two year college with a four year goal, make sure the four year college will accept transfer credits from the two year college prior to committing.

(2) CNBC David Faber's documentary entitled "The House of Cards"

Chapter 13

I was driving to work quite a number of years ago and scanning the radio stations within my range and landed on Howard Stern's morning radio program. Now I usually don't listen to Howard, but on this given morning, Howard is interviewing some guests and reminiscing about the 1960's. Howard, along with his cohorts, are talking to his guests about the people and times of an era long gone by. Toward the end of the segment, Howard says to one of his guests, but I am not sure who it was, "You seem to be doing very well for yourself many years after the 1960's have passed." His guest answers with the response, "Howard, after a while you figure out the system." Wow, isn't that the truth. Figure out the system and how Washington politics, the Wall Street complex, the educational system, and the military all interact, how funds are controlled and money flows between them. This is the key to how the power class is always one step ahead, or one generation ahead of the middle class.

Prior to World War II (1946) the power class went to four year college and the middle class did not. Then there was the G.I. bill whereby the middle class did go to college but then the power class was attending ivy league or high profile colleges. The middle class in the 1950's did not have many stock investments outside of the company that they worked for. The power class had investment portfolios and many times they were part of the high cost full service brokerage houses. The Individual Retirement Account (IRA) provided a way for the middle class to save and invest and spawned a plethora of mutual fund companies to satisfy the thirst for the middle class to invest, especially for retirement. The power class countered with superstar hedge fund managers that would only handle accounts with minimum investments well into seven figures. The middle class started to control some of their own stock investments and this demand created the niche for discount brokers. The power class has the control of the boards of public traded companies and the middle class has yet to crack that barrier so that the shareholders are truly the owners of the company. This is the good old boy system that permits the people at the top of a company to control the wealth even in the face of poor performance. The top administrators and board of directors can skim the cream, and owning shares of a good company is not necessarily dollars in your pocket. This is why I like companies that pay dividends when I invest in stocks.

There have been some mutual fund managers that have tried to gain seats on the board of directors of various companies, or in some way by controlling large numbers of shares, influence the decision making in favor of the shareholders. Warren Buffet comes to mind first, and also Michael Price did have some success at it when he ran the Mutual Series of funds.

I love it when the pundits on television say that the shareholders must oust these various CEO's and Boards of Directors. They have no more chance of controlling the excessive salaries of top executives and CEO's than they do of containing costs of private colleges. These are the bastions of the power class at the present time and they are not relinquishing it.

For years the IPO (initial public offering) of stocks new to the market was limited to a select group of clients. I can remember calling my broker at Merrill Lynch and asking about IPO's and was told that none of them were available to his office. There was an easy dollar to be made by keeping these IPO's for a few days and selling them, but it was restricted to pretty much the power class. New regulations and policies have made them more available, but they are much less profitable. It was a quick buck for a select few with little risk while it lasted.

One day, during the last weeks of August 2007, a large brokerage house had a meeting with four or five dozen or so of its most deserving clients and offered them the opportunity to trade on the investment tips presented. Obviously this generated an uproar among its excluded clients. The brokerage's response was very weak and said something about its excluded clients could suffer from information overload. Not only did the brokerage exclude them, could it be that it then insulted their intelligence? The last two weeks of August are usually somewhat sleepy on Wall Street and it was a good time to disseminate information. Sometimes "trading tips" to buy, sell or short a stock can in itself cause a blip that can be profitable. When someone can make a statement on television or in a newspaper that can alter the value of a company, we are walking a fine line of volatility. Buyer beware.

Chapter 14

One of the best sources of public information was Wall Street Week with Louis Rukeyser. This was a one half hour show that aired on national public television and lasted on public network for over 30 years. Rukeyser was bullish on the stock market when the Dow was wallowing between 800 and 1000. He presented a "reader's digest" version of the week in review. There were more pearls of wisdom collated into that one half hour than one can ever imagine. He unselfishly shared the thoughts and ideas of his high profile guests with his audience.

One evening he had Richard Bernstein from Merrill Lynch as a guest. At the time I was just starting to notice the construction of some Mc Mansions in our area. I also knew that many homes, no matter how expensive, had oil heat as the only option. I began to believe that the real estate market would drop before 2008, because of the high cost of heating fuel, not because of sub prime mortgage failure. Richard Bernstein's recommendation was Exxon oil which was about $42 per share at the time. I bought some Exxon and some British Petroleum. When they about doubled I sold half of what I had. I also bought and sold XLE which is an ETF of various oil stocks. Earlier I said, "know thyself." I know that I see things on a macro level; Wanda calls me a bottom liner. It probably has to do with the right sided vs. left sided brain thing that I talked about earlier. I am not good at picking individual stocks, but I am good at seeing things on a much larger platform. I knew that when Bush & Cheney were elected, we were not going to have a strong energy policy or one at all. So I was intent on finding a way to invest in energy. The policy of this regime was going to be "let the good old boys roll in the dough" with energy. Richard Bernstein confirmed my thoughts and I bought.

There are many books that show how the military, industrial and financial complex work on a micro level with explicit detail. They also confirm that one can "figure out the system" on a macro level. Public awareness is raised on a micro level, but public injustices are solved on a macro level.

I would be remiss if I didn't mention another person that is extremely knowledgeable and was a routine guest on Louis Rukeyser's television show. His name is Tom Gallagher and he is a political economist. Being assigned to Washington, DC, Tom was a wealth of knowledge and always presented a unique point of view. At one point in my life I made numerous trips across the Canadian border and on a personal level realized that every time I purchased some item in a Canadian store my purchasing power was less. I didn't know how to profit from this.

At about the same time, I was watching Rukeyser's New Year's show. This was where everyone dresses formally and each guest is allowed to pick stocks or other investments for the next year. No one could change their picks and the contest would be reviewed 51 weeks later and the winner announced. Tom Gallagher announced his portfolio of about ½ dozen items, but the most heavily weighted was the purchase of European dollars or euros. I was sure this was a winner and confirmed my feeling that the dollar was going to be worth less against the Canadian dollar and the euro. I tried every which way I could to purchase euros on an investment basis. At this point there were no ETF's like today, whereby you can purchase a variety of currencies from an online broker. I even called my full service broker and had him looking and the only thing he could come up with was a "Loomis Bond fund," not exactly where I wanted to go. Needless to say when the winner of the contest was announced, Tom Gallagher was the winner with a gain of over 80% and a huge part because of his euro purchase one year earlier. I had a new found respect for the term political economist and Tom Gallagher, but more important for my shortcomings. I was unable to cash in on my strong impression that the euro was going to rise in value to the American dollar.

Chapter 15

My biggest shortcoming in writing this book is that I painted the people working in the financial industry with a broad brush when in actuality it is a very narrow band of people that almost caused the collapse of the banking and financial industry. Although narrow, and mostly confined to the mortgage and banking industry, these are public companies owned by shareholders like you and me. There is a whole other entity of private equity risk takers that grow small business into larger ones and create the cradle of employment in this country. These people are the heart of real America. They use their own money and many times the money of family and friends to launch new companies or to grow small companies into larger ones. By no means is my intent to disparage private equity or portray any negativity on this group or any of the honest people that work hard in the financial or banking industry.

My feeling that when greed overtakes the welfare of public traded companies and endangers the fabric of our society, then it is an act of internal terrorism and, perhaps, that may be a bit harsh. But the effect can be devastating.

Louis Rukeyser was asked, when financial news hit the television screen 24 hours/day, why his program was only one half hour per week. His answer was quick and simple, "Why do you need more?" I am a one-trick pony. This is my only book and I fear that I may fall short in reaching my target audience. I wanted to reach high school teenagers and novice investors but most of all I want to leave my grandchildren with a guidepost for life.

I truly hope that I have. Not a lot of fluff or filler, but a lot of factual experience.

I also had a tendency to become really confident after I sold most of my stocks one month prior to the meltdown of 2008. That was quickly reversed. I am sitting in a car dealership waiting for an oil change around March 10, 2009. The stock market is really doing poorly and I flip on CNBC financial television news. Another man comes in and sits down and starts reading a magazine and I ask him if he wants to change to another television channel. His response really floored me. He told me that it is really a moot point because his financial advisor told all her clients to sell their stocks and go to fixed income one year before the meltdown. She worked for Wachovia Bank in Connecticut and met with her clients every six months individually and every three months met with them in small groups if they wished. He followed her advice and did very well. Now this advisor deserves to be a bonus baby if ever there was one.

I grew up in a mill town in upstate New York where they manufactured textiles prior to World War II. My handicap is that I review any money situation with a suspicious eye. I can remember being a teenager and seeing my friend's parents being laid off and unable to find work. The textile industry started to come apart in the 1950's when we were in high school. It was awful because these towns in the Mohawk Valley were one-industry towns.

Fortunately, my parents were not employed in these industries but to this day this area never participated in the financial expansion, prosperity and huge housing bubble that was enjoyed throughout most of the United States in the second half of the 20th century. The only silver lining to this situation is that they were spared from the housing bust of 2008. This area was the first area in New York State to really suffer high job losses with the textile industry leaving empty buildings for cheaper labor in the Carolina's.

All of us, even though we were kids, knew that our only chance of landing a good job was to study hard, go to college if we could, and move away. I don't think that in all the places that I have lived was there such an intense desire by parents to have their children move on for a better life. Mind you, other nearby cities outside of the Mohawk Valley were doing much better for employment. That was the 1950's and early 1960's, but the blight spread throughout the area west of Albany, the state capital. Buffalo had heavy industry like G.M. engines and transmission manufacturing; Rochester had Polaroid, Xerox, and huge Kodak employment; Ithaca-Cortland had Smith Corona which is now completely gone; Syracuse lost Transaxle and Transfer casing manufacturing along with most of Carrier; Binghamton-Endicott lost huge numbers of IBMers. The list goes on.

It is ironic that these cities are in the same state as New York City, the financial capital of the world where these multimillion dollar bonuses are a relatively common occurrence. It is also interesting that the Western New York area was one of the areas that least participated in housing appreciation in the whole United States. Lou Dobbs, the CNN show host, took his show on the road to Buffalo for several town hall meetings. It seems that politicians all visit upstate New York when they are running for political office, but it all ends there. No promises or commitments have resulted in stimulating employment in this area. Syracuse did get some new jobs with Lockheed Martin's participation in the war effort. But most of upstate New York is sliding inexorably into minimum wage jobs as the only ones available.

I guess Warren Buffet never scrutinized upstate New York when he admitted that he also thought that housing prices would only go up. (3) What were you thinking Warren?? I always felt that a house was a commodity, although a place to live. When Ross Perot said in the early 1990's that NAFTA (North America Free Trade Agreement) would produce a great sucking sound of jobs leaving America, I was already familiar with that sound from what I experienced in upstate New York in the 1950's..

(3) Warren Buffet being interviewed on CNBC television by Becky Quick

Chapter 16

Sometimes when we study the past in a completely objective way, we can see into the future. This textile area never really had the boom eras of say, the auto plants in the upper Midwest with their good union wages and benefits. There was very little housing bubble -- or any bubble whatsoever. Professionals did fairly well as did business owners. It was more difficult, however, to start your own business in an area where less expendable income was available. And no one was going to pay you a big salary to work for them or run their business. The Midwest had great employment times for many years post World War II, but of late it has fallen from favor. The textile industry in central New York never had high paying industry or managerial jobs, it pretty well was a two class society. Never forget where you came from because you can wind up there again if you are not careful. Never let your ego swell because this always puts you at a disadvantage in objectivity.

This writing was a lifetime study because of my passion for economics and my desire to leave a legacy to my grandchildren. To determine if you got your money's worth let's take Bernie Madoff for an example. Let's assume we know of his results but let us see if he would have fooled us as depression investors. We must remember that he fooled regular people like us, but that he also fooled people of the power class, some very smart wealthy business people. Let us see how this unfolds.

Madoff was born in 1938. At the time of his high school graduation the top students became medical doctors or lawyers. That was the standard of success at that time for his generation. The top notch people that went into other venues went to prestigious schools, Madoff did not. Two triggers here.

Depression investors would never put all of their money or the bulk of their money into one fund; many of Madoff's investors did. We would have only invested the interest or dividends from fixed income in his fund, not our seed money.

Yearly we would have asked for repayment of all interest and dividends not the principal. We would then decide -- compare them to the benchmarks and reevaluate where to invest our profits only.

We then would have looked at where he invested in stocks -- at least his top ten holdings as we did with Dodge & Cox.

Next we would match the stocks against all the sages we routinely review. See what they think about the allocations and/or individual stocks Bernie has purchased.

If you built an increasing value in Bernie's fund you would slide a portion of that over to fixed income. The percentage would be at your comfort level.

If something seems too good to be true, it probably is. When someone is consistently beating the odds, find out why. Are they lucky or taking on too much risk or lying?

Although Bill Miller of Legg Mason beat the S&P 500 for 15 consecutive years, he was heavily into financials (especially Lehman Bros.). When it crashed, his fund got hurt.

Use your triggers. Everyone has an area or business that they know something about. Relate your specific knowledge to something your stock picker purchases.

Watch out for overloading too heavily in one industry. Example -- perhaps Dodge & Cox Balanced was too overloaded in financials.

You are best off in mutual funds or ETF's unless you have specific knowledge of a specific stock or stocks.

Sometimes I will use a full service broker with good research access to confirm a purchase if I decide to buy individual stocks. It is worth the fee. Some discount brokers follow good research practices.

Remember that you may know more about a specific area than a so-called pundit or broker.

I like mutual funds with at least 30 but not more than 100 stocks.

I think if you invest in stocks, the Dow (30) index and several other large companies close to it will be the poster child for the United States. This will have to look good in order for the United States to borrow money on a global stage.

I do not like the S&P 500 stock index because I question the fact of whether there are 500 good stocks that I would want to hold in another severe downturn.

The stock market goes up and down, and it does not provide a constant even gain year after year such as Madoff did. Your fixed portfolio does level out the bad years for equities. What were Madoff's clients thinking? Be prepared for down years for your equity portion of your portfolio if you decide on equities.

Know your risk tolerance.

Know thyself -- your strengths and your weaknesses.

Use my own, or develop your own series of consultants to follow trends in the markets, including bonds, interest rates, etc. By the way, Jim Grant is a good source of interest rate trends.

When interest rates go up, the intrinsic value of bonds generally go down unless held to maturity. At maturity, the bond should pay the face value of the bond. In other words, you should get your money back on individual bonds. On bond funds, if you have to sell when the fund is down in value, you may lose money, so I prefer individual bonds and hold them to maturity. Investment grade bonds go from Triple A to Triple B, with Triple A being the most likely to completely pay you all of your money at maturity. This is the game I played to accumulate my seed money. I try to ladder out my bonds so they don't all mature the same year. I play what I think the interest rates will be for such and such a length of time and what the quality of the bond is. By laddering my maturity dates I can get some higher rates when some bonds mature and some lower rates when other bonds mature. Between the two I can usually average out a decent return. The returns are what I invest in stocks. Considering the amount of debt the Federal Government has, I figure by 2011 or 2012 we will see an increase in interest rates. At that point I will buy more bonds with various maturity dates.

At this point I think Bernie Madoff is getting hammered by the Depression Investor. Now there were some brokerage houses that would not deal with Madoff at all. One of their biggest contentions was his lack of transparency; in other words he wouldn't divulge his method of investing. Of course, in addition to this, the brokerage houses have more sophisticated modalities to detect fraud. So some brokerage houses had Madoff figured out, but you know what? My system will most likely help you. When anyone tells you that they, and only they, have the key to the magic potion and they lack transparency, beware, they ain't that smart! The chances that a business major from an average school that would rebuke medical school and other prestigious business schools, go to Wall Street and be able to outsmart all the Ivy League types and refuse transparency for his techniques and gains, is about as close to nil as one can get.

Keep a suspicious eye on anyone you give money to for investment. Always plan for the worst case scenarios.

Let us be clear. I am in no way advocating that you should buy stocks. If you decide to do so, you should seek professional advice at the time you decide to invest. I have gotten burned like many people when the tech bubble burst but I only nibble in equities. When the NASDAQ was around 800 I felt it was going to rise in value. I looked for an ETF that would mimic the Nasdaq. There was none. I looked at tech funds and bought two and got burned. I found one fund on the west coast that I liked but the expenses were too high. Finally QQQ was introduced that mimicked the NASDAQ. I bought 100 shares for $5629 on 4/9/99. I have been underwater on this for 10 years. I keep it just as a reminder. QQQ was purchased two weeks after it was introduced, but long after the NASDAQ was at 800. Timing is everything. So you can listen to all the noise on tech on television but in reality, except for a very few companies, the QQQ is down from 10 years ago. The day before 9/11/01 the Dow closed at 9605.51. On 9/11/09 the Dow closed 0.10 below the 9/11/01 figure. Not much of a gain for 8 years, but you would have dividends. If you bought the Dow Index on October 9, 2007 you would have paid $14,164.53 at its record close. The S&P was 1565.15, a record close on the same day. So with this in mind, you can have a reference point in stock investing.

Chapter 17

From the launching of the first Russian satellite -- Sputnik in October of 1957 -- Americans took up the challenge of the space race and put a man on the moon by July 1969. A twelve-year span of intense focus and American ingenuity produced a plethora of technology that even influenced medical advancements. Several years later the focus changed although the space program has continued on. For a short time we were the envy of the world.

Since about 1970 there has been an erosion in our attitude toward the importance of math, science and technology in our educational system as well as in our personal values. The sun may be setting on us as the leading economy in the world; soon we may only be another player. The value of our dollar has been slipping for many years and soon investors will hedge its downward slide with perhaps foreign bonds, gold or other commodities. It will become harder and harder to finance our government debt.

Our nation can become secure when we can destroy any rogue country's nuclear missile with our own antimissile missile on a consistent and predictable basis. This will only be achieved through science, math and technology. The next engine of growth for this country's economy will have to come through science, math and technology. Somewhere we must achieve the focus and determination that we exhibited between 1957 and 1969 when we landed on the moon. Financial engineering will not solve these problems.

We need to explore more about the physiology of intelligence. We test only such a small aspect of intelligence that we leave the bulk of it unexplored. I always think about a baseball player's hitting ability. We all have a dominant hand, we are called right-handed or left-handed. We also have a dominant eye. If your dominant eye is on the same side of your body as your dominant hand it would be called "ipsilateral" (same sided). If your dominant eye is on the opposite side as your dominant hand, it would be called "contra lateral" (opposite side). When a baseball can be thrown upwards of 90 miles per hour a batter's reaction time has to be measured within fractions of seconds, especially in the professional ranks. Keen eyesight in picking up the ball is critical as the ball leaves the pitcher's hand, and the quicker it can be visually identified the more time the brain has to process the necessary reaction. Contra lateral eye hand dominance would seem to be an advantage. In other words, a right handed batter would have his power stroke in his right hand. If he has a contra lateral eye hand dominance as he faces the pitcher, his left eye is closer to the pitcher and should pick up the ball earlier than he would if he is right eye dominant and right handed (ipsilateral). The opposite would be true for left hand batters. This is true in most cases but not always. Everything happens so fast. The brain receives visual stimuli and must process this information and transfer this information to a physical action of swinging the bat. This processing of information is very complicated but a form of intelligence that we haven't measured.

When I was 14 years old, I played baseball in a summer league that was composed of 13 and 14-year olds. One day I got a call from my Cousin Joe, who was one year older and played in the 15- and 16-year old league. Joe & I both had an Uncle Tony who was an excellent ball player and occasionally adults used to come up to me and ask me if I was related to Tony and then proceed to tell me what an excellent ball player he was. Joe & I each shared some of Tony's ability, but not all of it.

My Cousin Joe called one day and told me that his team's right fielder was sick and that they were short one player for the next day's game. They would have to forfeit the game if I couldn't fill in right field for them. After I told Joe that I would play, he said that Chico was pitching against us tomorrow. "Wait a minute - doesn't Chico play in that 16-17 year old All City League?" I asked. "Yeah, but when he pitches in this league and pitches a no-hitter he gets his name in the local paper," was Joe's response. Now I know Chico, he was a big guy, could really throw hard, and pitched on our school's varsity.

When I got to the field which was well kept, I noticed that the grass in right field was long. The field was all cut and trimmed, but it rained when they were cutting the lawn the day before and the grass in right field and right center had not been cut. It definitely will slow down my running. We took the field first and as I was playing right field I was a little worried about my speed and the long grass. No problem, nothing hit to right field the first inning.

Now it is our turn to bat. I know a lot of our players and they are pretty good. I watch Chico from behind the backstop. This guy Chico can really bring it, with strikeouts on the first two batters. Our batters are swinging when the ball is in the catcher's glove. Two strikeouts and my cousin Joe is up. Surely Joe, if anybody, can hit Chico. Joe fouls a couple off but his last swing is a foul tip and the catcher holds on and Joe is out.

Out to the outfield and the long grass, but fortunately nothing is hit my way. The bottom of inning two and I go to my place behind the backstop to study more of Chico. I notice he throws from right over the top and makes no attempt to hide the ball. Surely one of our guys will get a hit this inning. Not so, Chico is overpowering and three more batters go down without a hit. Now it's top of the third with the score tied zero to zero.

The top of the third was uneventful with no runs scored and no hits to right field. Our pitcher was hit a few times with scattered hits, but no runs scored.

Now it's the bottom of the third and I will be the third man to face Chico. The seventh and eighth batters were totally overmatched by Chico and struck out. Chico is really pumped by now and is only throwing fast balls. At this point I don't know anything about dominant eye or dominant hand coordination or have any idea how the brain processes information. I decide, before I go up to the plate, that I am going to take the first two pitches and try to hit the third pitch. At this point Chico just wants to throw strikes, get his no hitter and get this scrub ninth batter out, so he can get his name in the local paper. The first pitch he throws to me is a strike, the second pitch was a ball just off the outside corner. What I decided on the third pitch was to start swinging when the ball started to leave Chico's hand at the top of his delivery. When he delivers the ball, crack, I line to right center between the fielders. I was halfway to second base when I realized that the long grass was slowing the ball and I returned to first base. Clean hit, no doubt about it. Chico threw his glove down and walked off the mound. Since they only had nine players and Chico left, we won by forfeit. Everybody has 15 minutes of fame.

What does this all mean? I am trying to put this intelligence question of how smart people are on a different platform. There are many uncharted forms of intelligence that have to do with the neurotransmission of visual stimuli that can be processed by the brain and transposed to a neuromuscular function resulting in a programmed physical motion. Using various sports, I try to illustrate my point with examples that are familiar to all. When our whole team faced Chico's fastball, none of us could process our eye hand coordination fast enough to hit it (one form of intelligence). I figured out how to hit it by studying Chico's delivery and outsmarting him by selecting a pitch to hit prior to Chico throwing the ball (a second form of intelligence). Again, we all have skills and talents that we can use, don't ever give up and feel that you don't know anything about investing. Never give up and feel that the only forms of intelligence are the several ones tested by educators. Study hard and explore other talents you have; you may be pleasantly surprised.

While in high school I took trigonometry which was composed of, among other things, triangles and angles. I was very fortunate to have a teacher that was extremely bright. He graduated from the New York Maritime College with a degree in engineering, taught high school math for several years and then went on to a doctorate program in physics. It was during his high school teaching stint that I was fortunate to be his student. There was only one problem -- when I looked at the triangle and saw the various angles, I saw them in reverse or backwards. Now I never had this problem before in any other courses I had taken. But I figured out how to solve the problems, I did the problems using negative angles, in other words, I solved them backwards. When I presented my theory of negative angles to my teacher he did not squash or belittle my theory but instead he presented it to the director of the next teacher's math conference that he attended. After he returned, it was determined that I could solve my trigonometry problems with reverse angles. All turned out well. I now realize it was my right brained approach to solving problems. (Thank you Frank Collea.)

We must explore the other aspects of intelligence and the way the brain processes information. This may be the beginning of the next engine of growth that has been distinctive in our American culture and entrepreneurial spirit. One must always try to turn a disadvantage into an advantage. We must try to reach all children and encourage them to learn and develop.

All Ponzi schemes have a few common nuances. The Madoff scheme made the clients feel that they were among the select few that were allowed to participate in this profitable enterprise. Madoff appealed to their ego. He told them they would consistently earn more money with him than anyone else to appeal to their greed. Madoff then appealed to their intelligence by making them feel that they must be of superior intelligence to invest with him. If you are middle class, with him you were destined to be part of the power class. If you were already power class, you would be reaffirmed power class because you invested with him. Ponzi schemer's usually use eighth grade psychology to sell their products. Ego, greed and status are their bailiwicks.

Beware of things like "structured products," "derivatives," "packaged debt" and things that can't be easily explained or understood, and never believe housing is a form of savings. Always remember that debt is a form of servitude and if anything seems to be too good to be true it probably is.

I wish someone would have outlined a lifetime study that I could have used as a beacon for financial decisions when I was a young person - I would not have suffered all the bumps and bruises along the way. You don't have to have statistical sophisticated technical charts to arrive at the correct decision. You may arrive at the correct decision by common sense and observation. It only matters that you get there in time by whatever means.

So to my "Huckleberry" and my "Butterfly" and all you Depression Investors, I hope I have given you a sharp eye and a keen wit for your financial journey in your life.

Love, Grandpa

www.ingramcontent.com/pod-product-compliance
Lightning Source LLC
Chambersburg PA
CBHW020339290526
45785CB00005B/2092